Fatal Attractions

BOOKS IN THE PROTESTANT PULPIT EXCHANGE

Be My People: Sermons on the Ten Commandments
Ross W. Marrs

Be My Guest: Sermons on the Lord's Supper
C. Thomas Hilton

Believe in Me: Sermons on the Apostles' Creed
James H. Harnish

Fatal Attractions: Sermons on the Seven Deadly Sins
William R. White

What Are You Waiting For?
Sermons on the Parables of Jesus
Mark Trotter

Fatal Attractions

Sermons on the Seven Deadly Sins

William R. White

Abingdon Press
Nashville

FATAL ATTRACTIONS: SERMONS ON THE SEVEN DEADLY SINS

This book is printed on recycled, acid-free paper.

Library of Congress Cataloging-in-Publication Data

WHITE, WILLIAM R. (WILLIAM ROBERT), 1939-
    Fatal attractions : sermons on the seven deadly sins / William R. White.
        p.   cm.—(Protestant pulpit exchange)
    ISBN 0-687-12785-8 (alk. paper)
    1. Deadly sins—Sermons.   2. Sermons, American.   I. Title.   II. Series.
BV4626.W45   1992
241'.3—dc20
                                                                92-12749
                                                                CIP

Scripture quotations, unless otherwise indicated, are from the New Revised Standard Version Bible, copyright © 1989, by the Division of Christian Education of the National Council of the Churches of Christ in the United States of America.

Scripture quotations noted RSV are from the Revised Standard Version of the Bible, copyright 1946, 1952, 1971 by the Division of Christian Education of the National Council of Churches of Christ in the U.S.A. Used by permission.

"And God Said Yes!" is reprinted from FOR MATURE ADULTS ONLY by Norman Habel, copyright © Norman Habel. Used by permission of Augsburg Fortress.

"An Eye for an Eye," "The Poison Cake," and "The Treasure" are reprinted from STORIES FOR TELLING by William R. White, copyright © 1986 Augsburg Publishing House. Used by permission of Augsburg Fortress.

93 94 95 96 97 98 99 00 01 02 03—10 9 8 7 6 5 4 3 2

MANUFACTURED IN THE UNITED STATES OF AMERICA

To my mother,
Rhoda

Contents

PREFACE

9

INTRODUCTION

11

THE GREAT SIN: Pride

21

GRUMBLING AGAINST GOD: Envy

27

LET GOD FIGHT FOR US: Anger

35

FOREVER SPECTATORS: Sloth

41

GIVING UP OUR IDOLS: Greed

47

FOOD WITHOUT FRIENDS: Gluttony

53

SETTLING FOR SEX: Lust

59

A SECOND CHANCE: Ash Wednesday

65

GOD'S NO: Good Friday

71

GOD'S YES: Easter Sunday

79

Preface

From 1976-91 I served as the sole pastor of a Michigan congregation. There I preached fifty sermons a year, excluding weddings and funerals. Initially, I used only a traditional style of preaching, relying heavily on ideas and concepts.

Early in my tenure two discoveries led me toward a change in my preaching method. First, I became aware that the Bible uses a variety of literary styles to communicate the word. The Gospels report that Jesus used similes, metaphors, parables, and stories to help people imagine and understand his radically new teaching about the kingdom of God.

Next, the more I got to know people, the more aware I became of the diversity of my Sunday morning audience. Many of our people had postgraduate education, but a few had only finished eighth grade. We ranged in age from eighty-five years old to infants. Some of our people had solid biblical backgrounds, but others had never read an entire book of the Bible.

I soon determined that my approach to preaching needed to be as varied as the biblical texts and my audience. One style did not fit all. I began by using carefully selected folk tales and modern stories which illumined the lesson better than my traditional approach. At times I couldn't improve on the original, and I simply told the biblical story with a few words of explanation. Still other times I adapted a story from such sources as *Lest Innocent Blood Be Shed, Les Miserables,* or Edna Hong's *Bright Valley of Love.*

In 1986, with apologies to Garrison Keillor and his Lake Wobegon family, I began to offer an occasional narrative or story sermon revolving around a mythical town across Lake Michigan in my native Wisconsin. The response to these "stories from back home," was overwhelmingly positive. Weeks, even months later, I heard adults and children retell an entire sermon. "A Second Chance," which is found in this volume, is one of these story sermons.

In 1987, while on sabbatical, I became acquainted with the homiletical writings of Fred Craddock and Eugene Lowry. I began to reassess my use of story, attempting to work closely with the text, while still kindling the imagination. In this volume the methods used in "The Great Sin" and "Grumbling Against God" reflect this commitment.

In addition to the poets and the novelists who are acknowledged in the text, I am indebted to the exegesis of Charles Talbot and the late Bruce Schein and to the essays of William F. May and Henry Fairlie. Charles Gavin and Walter Bouman read major portions of the manuscript and offered helpful advice, too much of which, I fear, was ignored.

I do not advocate abandoning the traditional method of preaching. It often meets the needs of both the preacher and the text. However, it is not the only way to present the truth of the gospel. I am convinced that if we preachers are to proclaim a word that comes to us in a variety of literary styles to listeners diverse in education, age, and backgrounds, we will need more than a single arrow in our preaching quiver.

William R. White

Introduction

> If we say that we have no sin, we deceive ourselves, and the truth is not in us. (1 John 1:8)

In the Middle Ages a group of men and women in the Eastern monastic movement sought to love God with all their hearts, all their souls, and all their minds. In order to do this, they reasoned, they first needed to know the Word of God. They needed to let the Scriptures become a part of their breathing, for it was through the Word that God was revealed.

Their search did not stop with the Word for they not only wanted to be aware of that which drew them to God, they wanted to know the enemy, that which drew them away from God. They felt compelled to understand sin in its most concrete form.

In order to be specific and to provide confessors a catalog of sins for their work, these monastics began to compile a list of what they called "the deadly enemy." These sins were deadly not because they were the most grave, but because they were originating sins. Out of these seven, (pride, envy, anger, sloth, greed, gluttony, and lust) they reasoned, other sins are generated. From sloth arises malice, rancor, cowardice, and despair. Anger leads to murder, arson, cruelty, and vindictiveness. Out of greed comes theft and blackmail. And from pride, the root of all evil, comes boasting, arrogance, and hypocrisy, as well as the other six sins.

In A.D. 415 John Cassian brought the monastic movement to Gaul from the East and introduced the notion of the deadly sins to the Western church. Cassian, like his predecessors, sought to understand sin because of its destructive nature.

It was Pope Gregory the Great (590–604) who gave the Seven Deadly Sins their present form. Like his predecessors, Gregory's intent was to provide a specific list of sins to assist spiritual warriors who wanted to fight the enemy. The Pope wanted his monastics to make confession in order that they could better hear the healing and cleansing word of absolution. Soon, however, the list of seven caught the attention of a large segment of the general population who found it helpful in their spiritual journey. Loving God and fighting evil was not the vocation only of a select few.

Proclaiming the Good News

The sheer variety of ways that the New Testament Epistles announce the good news of God is amazing:

[He] has broken down the dividing wall, that is, the hostility between us.
—Ephesians 2:14

Therefore, if any one is in Christ, he is a new creation.
—II Corinthians 5:17, RSV

The free gift of God is eternal life in Christ Jesus our Lord.
—Romans 6:23

There is therefore now no condemnation for those who are in Christ Jesus.
—Romans 8:1

12

For by grace you have been saved through faith, and this is not your own doing; it is the gift of God.

—Ephesians 2:8

We have an advocate with the Father, Jesus Christ the righteous; and he is the expiation for our sins, and not for ours only but also for the sins of the whole world.

—I John 2:1, RSV

Like the New Testament writers, the preacher's task is to find many ways of announcing the almost-too-good-to-be-true news that God loves us, forgives us, and has died for us. Through the proclamation of the gospel, faith is formed, people are freed, and love is nourished. John is right, we love because God first loved us (I John 4:19).

Our proclamation of the good news also awakens in the hearer an awareness of sin. Even as a knowledge of God's love brings us near, we become painfully aware of what pulls us apart. Like the early monastics, the more we experience God's grace, the more we want to eliminate anything that alienates us. We want to understand the enemy.

Thus the task of preachers is not only to announce the way of God, but to help people understand the ways that are not of God. We identify and name sin, not with a malicious pleasure, but in the great hope that God's Spirit will use our words for the joyous process that begins with confession and ends with reconciliation to our neighbor and to God.

Problems in Preaching

It is no easy task to preach on sin. The traps are everywhere. For example, at times a sermon intending to name the enemy quickly turns to scolding and moralizing, two methods that make people feel bad without leading them to repentance. More important, such approaches trivialize sin, making it sound like naughty behavior.

The preacher's biggest problem, however, is self-deception,

both on the part of the listener and the speaker. Most of us prefer to think of ourselves not as sinners, but as nice people who make occasional mistakes. Ironically, it is virtuous, decent people who are most susceptible to self-deception.

Shusaku Endo's powerful novel, *Scandal*, is the story of Sugaro, an award winning Japanese novelist who built a reputation as his country's finest Christian writer. According to a reviewer in the story, his books explored the dark side of life, "the evil, loathsome filthy acts of men."

Sugaro's works delighted some readers, while they puzzled and disappointed others. "Why you don't write stories that are nicer, more beautiful?" an old priest once asked him. Upon reflection, Sugaro's answer was, "True religion should be able to respond to the dark melodies, the faulty and hideous sounds that echo from the hearts of men."

Still Sugaro wrote as a spectator, as an observer of other people's darkness. His was a safe, decent life that revolved around moments with his work, his wife, and other writers. He was a good man who explored the shadows of others.

Then, without warning, a rumor began to spread that Sugaro had often been seen frequenting the peep shows and porno houses of Tokyo's red light district. Left unanswered, the rumor would destroy his reputation as a Christian writer.

Immediately he began to track down the source of the rumor, traveling to the district in question. There Sugaro made two discoveries which both shocked and overwhelmed him. First, he uncovered a doppelganger, an apparition who bore his exact likeness. It was a sinister figure that appeared to Sugaro somewhere in the distance, just out of reach.

Next, he discovered that not only was the apparition something outside him, but it was also something that lived inside him. He discovered a self whose dark side made the sins he had spent his career writing about seem trivial. All his life he had underestimated the power of "the dark melodies, the faulty and hideous sounds that echo from the hearts of men," particularly when they echoed from his heart. Though he had written about it often, he had not really faced the power of sin.

Nor have we. Preacher and hearer alike find ways to justify and delude themselves. Despite our sin we find ways to think of ourselves as basically good people. We reject the whole notion that we are sinners. Pascal was right. "Certainly nothing offends us more rudely than the doctrine of sin, and yet without this mystery, the most incomprehensible of all, we are incomprehensible to ourselves."

Scandal does more than reveal the power of self-deception; it tells us what happens when recognition of sin is the last word. In one of the book's last scenes, Sugaro attends worship on the Sunday after Easter in a small rural church. Beyond the altar he sees an emaciated man with his arms spread wide. He hears the crowds jeering the man and finally he sees them throwing stones. Sugaro wonders, had he been present, if he too would have thrown a stone. Then quickly, Endo tells us that Sugaro went back to his office.

Is that all? Is there no change? The author seems to tell us that Sugaro has moved to recognition, but not to confession. He stopped just short of the final destination.

In preaching, our goal is not just to bring people to recognition or to inform, as if knowing the names of the sin are enough. Our purpose is to announce the good news that we have already been forgiven. A true hearing of the gospel leads to recognition *and confession*. And confession leads to the blessed word of absolution.

A Story

For fifteen years Ross had the Midas Touch. Every business venture, every deal he closed, every store he opened, turned into pure gold. His name was synonymous with success in his small community.

But the day Ross entered the pastor's office, he looked like a broken man. A few weeks earlier a part of his world had come tumbling down. His wife had discovered he had been sexually involved with an employee and she had confronted him. The confrontation led to a confession that there had been many women over the past decade.

"I want you to know," Ross began, "that I have appreciated the church very much. I admire your preaching and your leadership." He then began to tell his story.

When he finished the pastor asked Ross several questions. Finally he asked, "You have been a son of the church. You have been here almost every Sunday. You know the commandment regarding adultery. Did you see what you did as wrong?"

The man stared straight ahead before he answered. "No. I do now, but I have lived almost free of guilt these past years. I'm not sure I totally understand it myself, but I guess I just didn't think the commandment applied to me."

During the next few weeks, at the pastor's urging, Ross went into counseling. After several months he returned. "I appreciate the help I'm receiving from my counselor. But something is missing."

"Do you know what that something is?" asked the pastor.

He shook his head slowly. "No. No, I don't. I feel like I am making progress, but I feel worse now than I did when we began. I made a terrible mistake," Ross continued. "I hurt my wife, my children, and my friends. And I have told them so. Still, I have a terrible emptiness."

The two men talked for over an hour. Before Ross left, the pastor scheduled a time for them to get together the next week. At that session the pastor began by inviting Ross to bring him up to date. "What has happened since the last time we were together?"

"Not much," Ross began. "I've seen the counselor once. I continue to mend some broken fences. We haven't talked all that much, but I think my wife knows I feel terrible about the mistake I made. The kids are OK. I may be the only one who isn't getting better. I've done what I could and it doesn't seem to be enough."

After a few moments of silence the pastor spoke, "Ross, have you thought about the difference between making a mistake and committing a sin?"

The man looked baffled. "What do you mean?"

"I mean, yours was not merely a mistake, like a simple mathematical miscalculation. You knowingly broke your wedding promise to your wife and transgressed the limits God set for you in marriage. You acted as if you were immune from the command to be faithful. By your own admission, you saw yourself as above the law. You sinned against both your wife and God. What are you going to do about it?"

Ross began to protest, but instead he lapsed into reflective silence. Finally, he spoke. "You're right. I don't think I've come clean with anyone. I don't even know where to begin."

The pastor said simply, "If you wish to make a confession, I'll listen."

Ross looked confused. "Like they do in the Catholic Church?"

"Something like that," the pastor said as he opened a book to a service called "Individual Confession and Forgiveness."

The man looked it over carefully and then said, "How do we start?"

The pastor led him in reading a psalm. Then the two men prayed before the pastor invited Ross to make confession. At first there was an awkward silence. Then words flooded out, like water over a falls. Pain, tears, and deep emotion were released. Finally, after nearly twenty minutes, he was silent.

The pastor moved forward, placed his hands on Ross's head and spoke the healing words of forgiveness, "In the name of Jesus Christ, who said, 'Whatever you forgive on earth will be forgiven in heaven,' I declare the entire forgiveness of all your sins." The two men then sat together without speaking for another fifteen minutes.

A week later Ross was back. "I'm still seeing the counselor," he told his pastor, "but the logjam is broken. I was trying to handle things as if I made an error in judgment, when my real problem was I had sinned against God and my wife. I needed to name my sin and to confess my adultery. I believe I am on the right track with God. I'm also ready to make a full confession to my wife. Will you help me think about it?"

One of the reasons preachers have avoided preaching and teaching about sin is that they perceive it to be too negative. Perhaps they live with images of Puritan preachers condemning their fragile congregations.

When viewed from the goal, which is absolution, facing sin is far from a bleak experience. Repentance is not a matter of giving up the good things of life, but rather a turning that leads to God. Confession, which may include a painful inventory, ultimately leads to wholeness and health. Behind all preaching on sin is the promise, "If we confess our sins, he who is faithful and just will forgive us our sins and cleanse us from all unrighteousness" (I John 1:8, 9).

Fatal Attractions

PRIDE

The Pharisee, standing by himself, was praying thus, "God, I thank you that I am not like other people: thieves, rogues, adulterers, or even like this tax collector. I fast twice a week; I give a tenth of all my income." But the tax collector, standing far off, would not even look up to heaven, but was beating his breast and saying, "God, be merciful to me, a sinner!" I tell you, this man went down to his home justified rather than the other; for all who exalt themselves will be humbled, but all who humble themselves will be exalted.
(Luke 18:11-14)

The Great Sin

I f the events in the Parable of the Pharisee and the Tax Collector happened today I expect the Pharisee would find someone to plead his case before the public. It might go something like this:

"Good Morning. My name is Wellington David Cook III, president of the W. D. Cook Company, the oldest and largest public relations firm in the state. Our clients include some of the finest individuals and corporations in the nation.

"I have asked your pastor for just a few moments to right a wrong most ministers continue to inflict on one of my most outstanding clients, Amos ben Jonas.

"By a strange quirk of fate, Amos was included in the parable you read this morning. He is named only by his religious tradition, 'A Pharisee.'

"The parable tells you that my client went to the temple to pray. Unlike some people who only go to worship when they are in trouble, it is the practice of Amos to pray in the temple every day. Amos is a very devout and decent man.

"Some have criticized his prayer that begins, 'God, I thank you that I am not like other people.' Please note, Amos is merely reciting a prayer that is a part of his liturgy, a prayer all Pharisees pray. It is a prayer that some of you have prayed too, for its roots can be found in the Bible's oldest prayer book."

> If you try my heart, if you visit me by night,
>   if you test me, you will find no wickedness in me;
>   my mouth does not transgress.
> As for what others do, by the word of your lips
>   I have avoided the ways of the violent.
> My steps have held fast to your paths;
>   my feet have not slipped.
>   —Psalm 17:3-5

"Why is it that people say my client is proud and arrogant, but fail to make the same accusation against the very one he quotes, the psalmist? God has called us to be a holy people and Amos, like the psalmist, is making a simple point: he has made a great effort to be a holy and faithful man.

"Can anyone really doubt that what he says about being more faithful than the Tax Collector is true? Some of you may not like the comparison, but tell me, do you know the background of the Tax Collector? Do you know that like all tax collectors he has made a fortune by extortion and dishonesty? Do you know that he is a Jew who accumulates his wealth by collaborating with the hated Romans? He has used Roman soldiers to confiscate property and goods when people were unable to pay his so-called taxes.

"Before you make the Tax Collector a saint, remember that prior to the events of this parable he had not darkened the door of the synagogue in years. Then one day he comes in, sobs, cries out for mercy, and suddenly becomes a hero.

"By contrast, Amos loves his country and serves his church. I ask, which man do you want as a role model for faith?

> *"If God rewards crooks and castigates honest folks, what is the advantage of virtue?"*

"I don't know why Jesus seems to be so upset with Amos and others of the Pharisee party. Most people fast one day a week. Amos fasts two days. He also tithes. I ask, wouldn't most churches be overjoyed to have a liberal giver like Amos in their congregation? In addition, his reputation as a businessman is beyond reproach. He is honest in all his dealings.

"What kind of a religion is it that turns things upside down by praising rogues and slandering decent people? If God rewards crooks and castigates honest folks, what is the advantage of virtue?

"Finally, what is the value of religion? Amos is a religious man, spiritually superior in every way. The Tax Collector seldom worships, prays, or shares his wealth. Why is it that he went away justified rather than Amos? You be the judge. Quite frankly, I think Jesus blew this one."

If Mr. Cook were to make such an address, we would have to agree with almost everything he said. Pharisees were moral, upright members of the community. They were deeply religious and they were honest.

Tax collectors, on the other hand, were often scalawags. They were disloyal to their country and often to their religion. They created personal wealth at the expense of their other Jewish brothers and sisters.

The Pharisee is guilty of only one sin. But that sin is

what C. S. Lewis has called "The Great Sin." "By comparison," Lewis writes in *Mere Christianity*, "unchastity, anger, greed, drunkenness are mere fleabites." The sin is pride.

You and I know pride. We know it in others. We know the man who brags about anything and everything he has accomplished, the athlete who declares himself to be the greatest, the woman whose clothing or walk accents her vanity, the scholar who finds every opportunity to exhibit her mental superiority.

> *"Pride is a swelling of the heart filled with self-importance."*

We know pride. We hear those who boast of their fortune, their intelligence, or their skill. As the years pass we hear them boast endlessly about their children or their grandchildren.

But I know pride best by looking at myself. When I become irritated at someone who has corrected me, when I get upset with someone for dominating (that usually means I wanted to be center stage and they beat me to it), when I am offended because someone didn't fully acknowledge my contribution, my insight, or my hard work—it is my pride that has been piqued.

Let us be clear, pride is different than self-worth. It is different than self-esteem. Pride is self-esteem at the expense of other people. It is self-worth turned haughty, arrogant, and selfish.

Pride is a swelling of the heart filled with self-importance. It raises me up above others until I begin to look down on them. It is a spiritual cancer, eating up the possibilities for friendship, love, and community.

Pride is a sin, a deadly sin. It is the sin that stands

behind Hitler's war on the Jews, apartheid in South Africa, and racism everywhere. In every case, pride causes people to believe they are inherently superior to other people created in the image of God.

Pride is all these things, and more. For finally, the terror of this sin is that it is rooted in idolatry and unbelief. It not only elevates a person above others, but attempts to make that person equal to God. The tempter lures Adam and Eve toward the fruit by saying, "You will not die; for God knows that when you eat of it your eyes will be opened, and you will be like God, knowing good and evil" (Gen. 3:4-5).

> *"The terror, the deadly nature of sin, is that it separates us from God."*

The Pharisee in the story was so smug and self-satisfied that he needed and asked nothing from God. By his noble life, his morality, he could make it on his own. Why rely on grace when he was justified by his own efforts? Along the way he assumed the prerogatives of God, judging himself righteous and superior to the Tax Collector. What appears at first glance to be faith is really spiritual arrogance. Charles Talbert notes that "faith never expresses itself as despising others."

The terror, the deadly nature of sin, is that it separates us from God. This is true of any sin, including what we refer to as innocent little lies. Pride is the "Great Sin" because it destroys even those of great moral strength. It turns the finest fruit bitter. It attacks us, like the Pharisee, not at our weakness, but at our strength. Often we have admired a person of great ability or learning from afar, a person of great talent or courage. But our meeting with that person turns sour because we find him or her to be arrogant and conceited. Pride, writes Dorothy Sayers, is "the sin of the noble mind."

The Tax Collector is a despicable and pathetic person. He is not trusted by his own people, the Jews, or by his employers, the Romans. His situation seems hopeless. If he continues to live as a traitor to his people he is cut off from his friends, his country, and his religion. If he repents, he must make restitution for every drachma he has received by fraud, plus one fifth. And he loses his livelihood. His outburst is a genuine cry for mercy. He comes empty-handed, ready for any crumb that will fall from the Master's table. Yet he is the one who goes home filled, because he came empty. "Blessed are the meek, for they will inherit the earth" (Matt. 5:5).

Any honest searching of our heart quickly turns up a field of weeds. We sin against God and our neighbor. Our only hope is that the wonderful love and grace of God will wipe us clean and make us whole.

Two people went up into the temple to pray. Each received what he asked for. The first told God how good he was. He asked for nothing and received it. The second, deeply aware of his sin, cried out for mercy. And mercy was given.

You are free to do likewise.

ENVY

For the kingdom of heaven is like a landowner who went out early in the morning to hire laborers for his vineyard. (Matt. 20:1)

Grumbling Against God

*I*n the startling parable of the workers in the vineyard, we are told that the owner paid all of his employees the same wage, though many worked a different length of time, ranging from twelve hours to a single hour. Matthew reports that those who worked the entire day through the scorching heat grumbled when they received the usual daily wage. Do you think the explanation of the owner satisfied them? My hunch is that they filed a grievance before the National Labor Relations Board. Let's listen in on the proceedings.

Judge: "This special meeting of the National Labor Relations Board will now come to order. The first case is The People vs. Levi bar Jonas. The attorney for the plaintiff may call his first witness."

Attorney #1: "Your honor, we wish to call Eliezer. Eliezer, how old are you?"

Eliezer: "I am 26 years old."

Attorney #1: "And are you in good health?"

Eliezer: "I'm in excellent health. I haven't missed a day of work in five years."

Attorney #1: "Eliezer, tell this hearing where you were one week ago at 6 A.M."

Eliezer: "I was at the town square. Everyone who wants to work in the grape harvest meets there six days a week. We arrive early and wait for employers to come looking for workers."

Attorney #1: "Is this your first harvest?"

Eliezer: "No, sir. I have been working in the harvest since I was 14."

Attorney #1: "And on the day in question, did you find work?"

Eliezer: "Yes, sir, I did. At about 5:45 A.M. Mr. Levi, who has a large orchard, arrived in the square. Eight of us were there and he hired all of us."

Attorney #1: "Did you agree on a wage?"

Eliezer: "We did. He agreed to pay the prevailing wage, a silver coin. We expected to be paid at the end of the day, which was about 6 P.M."

Attorney #1: "Did the eight of you work alone all day?"

Eliezer: "No, sir. A little after 8 A.M., we told Mr. Levi that there were a lot more grapes than we could pick in a day. We told him some would rot if we didn't get help. He left and came back about 9 A.M. with a few other men. The same thing happened at noon and again at 3 and 5 P.M. I don't know why he hired the last two groups. We really didn't need them. By that time most of the work was done."

Attorney #1: "So how long did the others work?"

Eliezer: "It's easy to figure out. Some worked nine hours, some six, some three, and a few worked only one hour. The eight of us worked twelve hours, right through the hottest part of the day."

Attorney #1: "Tell the NLRB how the men were paid."

Eliezer: "Well normally, those that work longest get paid first. For some reason, Mr. Levi had Amos—that's his manager—pay the men who came at 5 P.M. first. He paid them a silver coin. He paid the same to the workers who came at 3 P.M. The eight of us who worked twelve hours figured we were going to get a bonus. When he came to us, he paid us a silver coin."

Attorney #1: "Do you think you were wronged?"

Eliezer: "You're darned tootin' we were wronged. He made the others equal to us and we worked eleven hours more."

Attorney #1: "Levi says he can do what he wants with his money. What do you say?"

Eliezer: "I say we got laws against such things. Whoever heard of a man working one hour getting the same wage as one who worked twelve? Next time I'll show up at 1 P.M."

Attorney #1: "I don't think there are any more questions at this time."

> *"Jesus is not telling Burger King or General Motors how to hire."*

How do you suppose this case is going to come out? Can the owner do what he wants with his money or will the NLRB declare that his is a public business and that he has to pay "fair wages"? If he insists on continuing this method of payment, will any men work for him the full day when they can work less for the same amount? If you were Eliezer, would you feel cheated?

Let's be clear, this parable is not about business; it is about the kingdom of God. As a way of conducting business, this parable may be sheer nonsense, but in the kingdom of God it is a marvelous gift. Jesus is not telling Burger King or General Motors how to hire, he is describing how God provides enough for everyone, even those unable to work the full day. If this seems outrageous it is because the love of God is outrageous.

By its very nature love does not keep score. It cannot. Special circumstances—poor health, unemployment, a recent catastrophe—mean that love gives more to one person than to another. Love responds to need; it is not calculating.

But if love is not calculating, envy is. The workers agreed to the normal day's wage, a silver coin. They received a silver coin. The problem was not their wage but the comparison. They would have been content with the identical wage if others received less.

This, then, is the first characteristic of envy. It is highly competitive; it is always comparing. A chilling Jewish folk tale tells of two merchants who owned shops across the street from one another. Each judged the day successful not on the basis of total sales, but on whether he made more than the other. Upon the completion of a sale, each would look across the street and mock the other. God decided to put an end to this nasty rivalry and sent an angel to visit one of the merchants.

"You can have anything you want in the world," the angel said. "It can be riches, wisdom, a long life, many children. Just know that whatever you ask, your competitor will get twice as much. Thus, if you ask for $20,000, he will get $40,000. What is your wish?"

The merchant thought for a while before he answered, "Make me blind in one eye." Envy is as senseless as that.

> **"By its very nature love does not keep score."**

Second, envy is known for its sounds, murmuring and grumbling, the sounds of discontent and dissatisfaction. These are irritating and corrosive sounds that eat away at others and the envious person.

Third, envy is blind to its own gifts. The envious person may have many wonderful assets and abilities, but all she can see is the gift she doesn't have. What others have always seems larger and more special than what the envious person has. Envy makes us blind to what the goodness of God has done for us.

Finally, envy creates sadness. Gone is a sense of thanksgiving and joy. How can we be thankful when we are only aware of what we don't have?

> *"When we can see our own gifts as clearly as we see the gifts of others, we have already moved away from envy."*

Jesus teaches his followers to be content with what they have. "Consider the lilies of the field, how they grow," he says. He opens their eyes to the goodness of God by looking first at the grass and flowers as a lesson. If God has gifted grass and flowers, how much more has God given gifts to his people?

The person of faith lives with a sense of delight and joy because that person believes life is a gift. Alleluia, not grumbling, is the sound of the thankful.

In another biblical story (Matt. 20:20-28), the mother of two of the disciples of Jesus, James and John, asks for special privilege for her sons. "Let them sit, one at your right hand and one at your left when you come into your kingdom," she asks. When the other ten disciples hear the request, they are filled with envy. How dare these two try to worm their way into the good seats?

Jesus heard the murmuring and used the opportunity to teach them about discipleship. He began by suggesting they replace envy with service. "You know that in other cultures the people who are great lord it over others," he said. "It will not be so among you. Whoever wishes to be great among you must be a servant and whoever wishes to be first among you must be your slave." Then he concluded with a summary of his own ministry. "For the Son of Man came not to be served but to serve and to give his life as a ransom for many."

We will not end envy by trying harder. We put envy behind us when we allow God to take our grasping, possessing hearts and replace them with grateful, thankful hearts. It is all a matter of seeing. When we can see our own gifts as clearly as we see the gifts of others, we have already moved away from envy. Our journey continues when our grumbling is replaced with hymns of praise, sung in gratitude for all God has done for us.

Judge: "Does the attorney for Mr. Levi wish to cross examine Eliezer?"

Attorney #2: "We do, your honor. Eliezer, would you tell the court again what wage you agreed to work for?"

Eliezer: "A silver coin."

Attorney #2: "And what wage did you receive?"

Eliezer: "Don't start getting fancy with me."

Judge: "Eliezer, just answer the question."

Eliezer: "I received a silver coin."

Attorney #2: "Then surely you don't have any quarrel with Mr. Levi. You received the very wage you agreed upon."

Eliezer: "It isn't what I got. It is what they got that hurts. Either way it was unfair. Mr. Levi made them equal to those of us who worked longer hours."

Attorney #2: "So, you are not upset with your wage. You are upset with the wage of the other workers?"

Eliezer: "Doesn't anybody understand? Not only did we work longer hours, we did more and better work."

Attorney #2: "Please explain."

Eliezer: "Why do you think no one hired those other guys? Most of 'em are old and they have health problems. Bad backs and bad legs mostly. They can't keep up with us young guys. Mr. Levi gave the poor workers the same as the good workers."

Attorney #2: "Mr. Levi says that he was fair with you and generous to the others. Isn't he allowed to do what he chooses with what belongs to him?"

Eliezer: "It shouldn't be at my expense."

Attorney #2: "Mr. Levi says that he will not pay more than the prevailing wage. He offered and paid you a silver coin. That won't change. What is your solution?"

Eliezer (ponders before speaking): "Take away at least half of the wages of the others."

Attorney #2: "We rest our case, your honor."

ANGER

You have heard that it was said to those of ancient times, "You shall not murder"; and "whoever murders shall be liable to judgment." But I say to you that if you are angry with a brother or sister, you will be liable to judgment; and if you insult a brother or sister, you will be liable to the council; and if you say, "You fool," you will be liable to the hell of fire. (Matt. 5:21-22)

Let God Fight for Us

Pastor Jones was a controversial figure. His supporters described him as an enthusiastic and spirited speaker. His critics described him as angry and emotional.

In his congregation there was a small woman who spoke with a sharp Norwegian accent. She was alarmed at the pastor's emotional sermons and frequently said things like, "Vel, I tell you, calm down." One Sunday, following a "spirited" presentation on the issue of race, the woman met the pastor at the door with a pointed finger. "Anger becometh not a godly man," the woman hissed.

"But Lena," the pastor protested, "even Jesus got angry. One time he got so mad he even threw the money-changers out of the temple."

The woman considered the pastor's words for a moment and then said, "Yah, I know. But dats one ting I don't like about Jesus."

Many people have been on the receiving end of anger and, like Lena, are most uncomfortable in its presence. Anger has caused a lot of suffering. Yet, like death and taxes, anger just won't go away. It is present in our world and even associated with God in the Bible. There are over forty Old Testament references to the wrath of God. In the New Testament, Jesus not only overthrew the tables in the temple where money was changed and pigeons sold, he cursed a fig tree, causing it to wither.

Think of other biblical displays of anger. The book of Exodus tells how Moses carried two tablets of stone down the mountain only to find the people of Israel singing praises to a golden calf. Incensed with his people's infidelity, he flung the tablets to the earth, then ground the golden image to powder, scattering its remains upon the water. Was this a temper tantrum?

In the Psalms, the book we associate with hymns of praise and poetic prayers thanking God for his steadfast love and his mighty deeds, the writers often express anger. Listen to the concluding verses from Psalm 137: "O daughter Babylon, you devastator! Happy shall they be who pay you back what you have done to us! Happy shall they be who take your little ones and dash them against the rock!"

What do you suppose Lena thinks about Psalm 137? I'll tell you what a lot of churches think. They either eliminate the entire Psalm from their liturgies and worship books or simply omit these last two verses.

> *"Anger directed toward evil and injustice can be of God. It may even be a prerequisite for justice."*

Anger can be frightening, but we are asked neither to pretend it does not exist nor to let it run wild. There are both appropriate and inappropriate uses of anger.

Scripture suggests that God's anger is directed toward evil and injustice. The prophet Amos wails against "the cows of Bashan . . . who oppress the poor, who crush the needy, who say to their husbands, 'Bring something to drink!' " (Amos 4:1) and against those who "afflict the righteous, who take a bribe, and push aside the needy in the gate" (Amos 5:12). Amos says God, who witnessed Israel's evil treatment of the poor, is not impressed when they sing hymns and attend worship. "I hate, I despise your festivals, and I take no delight in your solemn assemblies. Even though you offer me your burnt offerings and grain offerings, I will not accept them" (Amos 5:21).

Nor is this understanding limited to the Old Testament. Paul, writing to the Romans declares, "For the wrath of God is revealed from heaven against all ungodliness and wickedness of those who by their wickedness suppress the truth" (Rom. 1:18). Anger directed toward evil and injustice can be of God. It may even be a prerequisite for justice, for unless we are angry when people are treated inhumanely, the condition will continue. It was not until African Americans became enraged over the Jim Crow laws in this country that they took to the streets in large numbers and began the process that led to social change.

One of my daily prayers goes like this: "God let me love what you love and hate what you hate." Lena may not like that prayer, but it recognizes a a legitimate use of anger.

And yet, anger is deadly. Without control, anger leads to bloodshed, pain, and death. Left unchecked, anger begins the cycle of violence. Folk literature warns us often about unchecked anger.

Many years ago in Lithuania a gentle old woman lived alone in the woods. On the rare occasion when she spoke to people it was always in proverbs that either baffled or irritated them.

She was particularly caustic to a rich landlord who lived in town for she thought him to be a lazy man. When she saw him sitting in the sun she said, "As a door turns on its hinges, so a sluggard turns on his bed." He hated the old woman.

One day the woman came upon the lord in the midst of a fierce argument. She moved between the shouting parties, pointed her finger in the landlord's face, and said, "A hot-tempered man stirs up strife, but he who is slow to anger quiets contention." The landlord was furious and vowed he would get rid of the meddling old woman.

When the woman next visited town the rich lord baked a cake full of poison. After talking with her in a friendly fashion, he offered her the present. "You have never tasted cake like this before," he assured her.

The woman's only words to the landlord were, "One day you will find yourself."

As the woman walked down the road with her cake, the man muttered to himself, "Today you will find yourself in the arms of death."

On the same day that the old woman visited the landlord, his young son participated in a hunt in the woods close to her home. He and his servants lost their way and soon found themselves outside the hut where the old woman lived. The young man knocked on the door and told the woman how hungry and thirsty he was. Immediately she invited him to have a piece of cake, which had not been touched. The young man fell to the ground dead after the first bite. The servants left immediately to bring the father. As he knelt before the body of his son, tears streaming down his cheeks, the old woman spoke again, "The man who makes holes falls into them himself."

Anger is included in our list of sins because, unleashed inappropriately, it *is* deadly. Anger, as in "I hate you," is akin to saying, "I wish you were dead." Alas, the rocketing homicide rates in our cities have taught us it is a short trip from anger to murder.

What do we learn about anger from the life of Jesus? First, we learn that Jesus was moved to anger by injustice. When he acted in anger, it was directed to tables and fig trees, not people.

> *"The answer to anger is suffering love."*

The life and words of Jesus taught his disciples to absorb the anger of others and to let the cycle of violence end with them. Early in Israel's life the law attempted to curb the power of the strong. Israel's "eye for an eye" was to limit retaliation. If provoked, one could only retaliate in kind— an eye for an eye, a bullet for a bullet, a rocket for a rocket.

But Jesus went one more step. He asked his followers not to avenge. If your enemies strike you, turn the other cheek. The cycle of violence ends when the injured party forgives rather than retaliates. The answer to anger is suffering love. When Abraham Lincoln announced to his cabinet that he intended to forgive the southerners and restore the South as best as he could, Secretary of State Stanton challenged him. "Mr. President, I say we ought to destroy our enemies." Lincoln replied, "Mr. Secretary, do we not destroy our enemies when we make them our friends?"

Jesus reminds those who follow him that they should even abstain from the humiliating words, "You fool!" Sticks and stones may break my bones but names sometimes do greater damage. Name calling is often the prelude to violence.

Can we completely avoid anger? No. The writer to the Ephesians puts it this way, "Be angry but do not sin; do not let the sun go down on your anger, and do not make room for the devil" (Eph. 4:26).

Jesus, following the lead of the psalmist, invites us to give up our anger, our vengeance. Let God fight for us. Remember those horrible words we read earlier from Psalm 137, the words that made us wince? Note that the writers do not ask permission to take care of matters themselves. They do not ask permission to kill the Babylonians or their children. They ask God to even the score. They ask God to establish justice.

Jesus tells us to turn our anger over to God. Let God handle the hatred of others. In the last week of his life, Jesus faced the anger of the Sadducees, the wrath of the Pharisees, the rage of the Zealot patriots. It ended in death, the death of the innocent Son of God. His response? "Father, forgive them, for they do not know what they are doing" (Luke 23:34).

What do we do with our anger and the anger of others? We turn it over to God, who makes a cross out of it and uses it to save a broken world.

SLOTH

Forever Spectators

In Elie Wiesel's largely autobiographical novel, *The Town Beyond the Wall*, Michael, a young Jew who survived the Holocaust, traveled at great personal risk behind the Iron Curtain to his Hungarian hometown. Though his memory burned with images of the soldiers and police who had brutalized him and those he loved, Michael returned to satisfy his curiosity, not for revenge.

In a strange way he understood the brutality of the executioners and the prison guards. What he did not understand was the man who lived across from the synagogue, the man who peered through his window day after day as thousands of Jews were herded into the death trains, reflecting "no pity, no pleasure, no shock, not even anger or interest. Impassive, cold, impersonal."

There is a bond, Michael thought, between the brutal executioner and the victim, even though the bond is negative. "They at least belong to the same universe. But not so the spectator. The spectator is entirely beyond us, seeing without being seen, present but unnoticed."

He concludes, "To be indifferent—for whatever reason—is to deny not only the validity of existence, but also its beauty. Betray, and you are a man; torture your neighbor, you're still a man. Evil is human, weakness is human; indifference is not."

Wiesel's anger toward the spectator is not unlike God's response to the people of Laodicea. God could understand hot. God could tolerate cold. But lukewarm was out of the question.

The hot are human. The cold are human. The lukewarm seem neither. In "The Shield of Achilles," W. H. Auden insists that the lukewarm "have lost their pride and died as men before their bodies died."

We speak here of the ancient and deadly sin of *acedia*, a Greek word that literally means "no care." *Acedia* can be translated either "apathy" or, a more juicy word that I prefer, "sloth."

Sloth is the sin of the one-talent man in Jesus' story, a man who was entrusted to invest a small portion of the owner's fortune. Rather than lose the owner's gift, the one-talent man buried it in the earth. In the eyes of the Master, the man's sin is timidity, abdication, and irresponsibility.

In the eyes of our world, the one-talent man is simply being cautious. It would only be a matter of time, in a litigious society, before the case would be in the hands of an attorney. "Your honor," the attorney would say, "what appears to be irresponsibility is actually prudence. In today's economic climate the careful investor is the wise investor. Though the Master did not receive a return *on* his investment, he did receive a return *of* his investment.

"But our most serious concern is the sentence. It is far too harsh. According to the laws of this great state, a sentence must fit the crime. We ask the court, is it fair that a person who buries a single talent in the earth should be thrown into the outer darkness, particularly if there is weeping and gnashing of teeth? We contend that a man who buried his talent should not be forced to share space with the likes of Hitler, Caligula, and the inventor of artificial turf. We, therefore, petition the court to change the sentence to ten hours of community service."

Our generation is apt to discount the sin of the one-talent man because compared to murder, theft, or rape, apathy seems insignificant. We are more likely to be concerned about sins of commission. It is time to reconsider. It is time to understand that sloth is indeed a deadly sin.

> *"God could understand hot. God could tolerate cold. But lukewarm was out of the question."*

In his autobiography, *Inside the Third Reich,* Albert Speer confesses that he was so obsessed with the power of his position as Hitler's chief architect that he became blind to the slaughter of the Jews. Speer was, by all accounts, a brilliant man who did such a spectacular job of organizing Germany's industry that his efforts alone may have prolonged the war by two years.

Born of a prosperous and professional family, Albert Speer was a fine husband and wonderful parent. He was a liberal who certainly did not hate Jewish people. He saw his position in the Third Reich as a great professional opportunity. Though thousands were murdered or imprisoned before his eyes, Speer claims he was oblivious to the horrors going on all around him. He was just an architect doing his job. The name for this deadly vice is sloth.

People often confuse sloth with idleness. Some of the busiest people in the world are the most apathetic to those in need. Perhaps it is their very activity that causes them to

43

be blind to the hurts of both the people closest to them and to the world's wounded. Even caring people can be guilty of the sin of not caring. Pastors, for example, who help everyone who knocks on their door, often turn a deaf ear to the cries from their own families.

> *"Fear and bad theology cause people to bury their finest gifts."*

Sloth is the sin of disconnecting ourselves from the rest of creation, from the rest of the human family.

Sloth is a crowd of people turning their heads when a woman is battered on the streets of New York City.

Sloth is a chemical company pouring toxic waste into a landfill.

Sloth is well-fed Americans ignoring the needs of the poor and lonely in their own neighborhoods.

The environment is in terrible shape. Our air and water are polluted. Our technology is ripping a hole in the ozone layer. We are running out of places to throw our junk. Sadly, I am not saying anything we Americans don't know. We do not lack information. We lack inspiration. We obviously don't care. The sin is called apathy.

The story of the talents is our story. It tells us that fear and bad theology cause people to bury their finest gifts. The fear is that terrible things will happen if I fail. The bad theology is an assumption that our master, our God, is harsh. Put the two together and reasoning that causes paralysis goes something like this: "If the Master is harsh then I had best not make any mistakes. I'll bury the talent." Arising out of this theology is a generation of hollow people who live in fear and without hope.

There is another theology that produces quite a different kind of people. These people, entrusted with five and two talents, have a different image of the Master. They believe that though the Master has high expectations, he is not harsh. They know the Master to be one who is slow to anger and abounding in steadfast love. They know the Master to be one who pays a full day's wage even to those who work but an hour. They know the Master as the Good Shepherd who leaves ninety-nine sheep behind and searches for a single lost, timid lamb. They know him as the Waiting Father who welcomes his returning and wayward children with robes, rings, sandals, and a party.

The first group are what T. S. Eliot would have called hollow people, stuffed people, leaning together, headpieces filled with straw. Alas! The second are far from hollow, they are a people who have been filled by a compassionate God who gave himself for all. They are filled with the conviction that when they reach out to a person in need they not only meet one who is a brother or sister, but they encounter the living God.

All have been handed talents and choices. Some see the world as dark and the Master as harsh. They bury their talents in the ground. Others see a world awash in light, filled with grace and second chances. They risk their gifts with the certainty that one day, regardless of outcome of their investment, they will hear the words, "Well done, good and faithful servant."

GREED

> It is easier for a camel to go through the eye of a needle than for someone who is rich to enter the kingdom of God. (Mark 10:25)

Giving Up Our Idols

A man ran up to Jesus and gushed, "Good Teacher, what must I do to inherit eternal life?" Most teachers recognize the technique. "O, fount of all knowledge, O divine seer." It was a bit too much, and the man must first be disarmed— "Why do you call me good?" Next, like a good teacher, Jesus called the man to draw upon his own resources, to reflect on his own training: "You know the commandments."

He did. And he had kept them, from his youth. We discover him to be a sincere, pious man who had attempted to live not by his own rules but by the rules of God. Still, living by rules had left him empty. Being good was not enough. The man sensed that there was more, but what?

For many of us life is not so much a gift as a matter of setting goals and achieving them. Life is something to be accomplished, something one plans. The man had met his own goals. In the process he had remained his own master, his own judge and lord. This illustrates a problem for all of us, but perhaps more so for those who are gifted or wealthy.

Jesus looked at the man and loved ("agaped") him. His heart went out to him. The man was no fraud. He was sincere, and that is why the story is so chilling. Jesus then attempted to free him from his bondage with an analysis followed by five imperatives: "You lack one thing—Go, Sell, Give, Come, Follow!" The commands are interrupted by a promise: "You will have treasure in heaven" (Mark 17:21).

Jesus intended this to be a moment of great liberation. The man did not hear it that way. Jesus intended to meet his deepest need, his deepest longing. The man's life appeared to be a dream come true, but he senses a terrible void. He found that God was missing from the dream, and the void came because there was an idol located at the center of his existence. It was so firmly placed he could not or would not dislodge it. At the words of Jesus he was shocked, his countenance fell, and he left grieving. For the moment, the idol—wealth—had won.

By most standards in the world, I am a rich man. As such, I gasp each time I hear this story. If I come to Jesus to ask for an aspirin will he suggest radical surgery? If this is the way he treats the ones he loves, am I able to handle such affection?

> "Serving God is a two-handed call, and it cannot be done when we are hanging onto what we own with one hand."

During this initial encounter, many of the disciples, and perhaps some of you, were not involved in the story. The disciples had given up all they had to follow Jesus. Their possessions, compared to the rich man, were few. Greed, they thought, is a rich man's game. Unlike most of us, they were poor. Up to this point they had listened to Jesus address the problem of someone else. It was interesting, but not crucial. Now he turned to them. "How hard it will be for those who have wealth to enter the kingdom of God!" Huh? Again! "It is easier for a camel to go through the eye of a needle than for someone who is rich to enter the kingdom of God!"

Who among us has not dreamed of being rich? Who among us, even those who don't play the lottery, has not dreamed of winning it? Who among us has not wondered about inheriting a fortune? All of us think that a few extra bucks wouldn't change us. "I can handle it, Lord," we cry. "Give me a shot at it." It might even free us up to pursue true ministry. Elsewhere Jesus warned his disciples of the danger of gaining the whole world only to forfeit their life. Even after such a warning most people I know would take the risk.

People in the first century were convinced that wealth was a sign of God's blessing. Perhaps we still think that way. The bumper sticker reads, "If you are so smart, why aren't you rich?"

But for Jesus, wealth is a hindrance, not a help to discipleship. Serving God is a two-handed call, and it cannot be done when we are hanging onto what we own with one hand. Jesus does not say we should not serve God and money, he says we cannot. All too frequently we do not own things, they own us.

There was a demon who owned a large box of gold coins that he kept buried under an old house. One day he was ordered to leave that area for another part of the world. He would not be able to return for twenty years. What should he do with the treasure during his absence? If he hired a guardian it would cost a great deal of money. If he left it under the house someone could dig it up and steal it. At last he thought of a foolproof idea.

He took the treasure to the home of a miser. "Dear Sir," the demon began, "I wish to give you this gift before I leave the country. I have always been fond of you, and I pray that you will not refuse my offer. You may feel free to spend these gold coins however you desire. There is but one stipulation. Should you die before me I am to be your sole heir." The miser agreed to accept the gift, and the demon departed.

Twenty years later the demon returned home to find that the miser had recently died. He found the treasure and discovered that not a single coin was missing. He laughed, knowing the miser had been a guardian who did not cost a penny. Hear the moral to this story: Is it not true that when we hoard our money we are merely saving it for the demons?

> *"We no longer see greed as a sin. It is a goal."*

Greed is demonic. It is idolatrous. You shall have no other gods, the commandment declares. Greed replaces God with the things money can buy.

Perhaps the most dangerous aspect of greed in our day is that it is assumed. A man is offered $2.1 million a year to play baseball and he is offended! He takes his employer to arbitration and wins $3 million.

We no longer see greed as a sin. It is a goal. If you are really rich you can be on "Greedstyles of the Rich and Famous." Greed is in. Instead of producing revulsion, it encourages envy.

It ought not be so among us. Money and the love of money distorts our values and hinders our discipleship. Jesus tells us that we must root out everything in our lives that prohibits us from following him. In the case of the rich man, it was the things he owned. What is it with us—lust, pride, selfishness?

The challenge to rid ourselves of our greed is not

intended to be sad. It is meant to be joyful and freeing. It is only when we want to hang onto our idols and when we love them more than God that they become a burden. When that happens, we too go away sorrowful.

Like repentance, the call for us to give up the idols of our lives is intended to be liberating. It is the call to give up being caterpillars in order to become butterflies. Every now and then someone hears this call, understands what it is about and accepts . . . joyfully. In the Gospel According to Luke, the story of the rich man is followed by the story of Zacchaeus, a man who hears the call of Jesus and gives up the idols of his life.

Jesus was passing through Jericho. A man named Zacchaeus was a chief tax collector there, and he was rich. He was trying to see who Jesus was but could not because he was short in stature and could not see over the crowd. So Zacchaeus ran ahead and climbed a sycamore tree because Jesus was going to pass that way. When Jesus came to the place, he looked up and said to him, "Zacchaeus, hurry and come down; for I must stay at your house today." So he hurried down and was happy to receive Jesus. All who saw it began to grumble and said, "He has gone to be the guest of one who is a sinner." Zacchaeus stood there and said to the Lord, "Look, half of my possessions, Lord, I will give to the poor; and if I have defrauded anyone of anything, I will pay back four times as much." Then Jesus said to him, "Today salvation has come to this house, because he too is a son of Abraham. For the Son of Man came to seek out and to save the lost" (Luke 19:1-10).

Our Lord calls us to rid ourselves of all that binds us. When we do as he asks, true joy is found and we hear these great promises: "Today salvation has come to this house," and "You will have treasure in heaven."

GLUTTONY

Food Without Friends

In Nikos Kazantzakis's novel, *Zorba the Greek*, Alexis Zorba speaks to his young friend, the boss. "Tell me what you do with the food you eat, and I'll tell you who you are. Some turn their food into fat and manure, some into work and good humor, and others, I'm told, into God." Mealtimes for Jesus and the disciples fell into categories two and three. They were times of refreshment, joy, and communion. But in the days preceding our story their lives resembled twentieth century America. They were so busy coming and going that there had been little time to rest or eat a leisurely meal together. If they didn't slow down, their food would soon turn into fat and manure.

Jesus, who often escaped to a lonely or isolated place to reflect and pray, knew the value of time spent in retreat. Out of concern for his friends he said, "Come away to a deserted place all by yourselves and rest a while."

Quickly the group jumped in the boat and sailed to a deserted place. But the crowds, hungry for a word from

53

Jesus, ran ahead and were waiting for him when he arrived at his getaway spot. Theirs was a hunger that the Jewish religious leaders had failed to satisfy. In effect, they were leaderless, wandering aimless in the world. Mark tells us Jesus had compassion and taught them.

Compassion may be the best one-word description of the ministry of Jesus. Twelve times the Gospel writers use the word to explain his actions. They tell us it was compassion that moved Jesus to heal a man born blind, to cleanse a leper, and to raise a young man from death. In the story of the fishes and loaves, his compassion was aroused three times—when he saw the stressful lives of the disciples, when he viewed the crowd who were like sheep without a shepherd, and late in the day when they were about to faint from lack of food.

Jesus used the word compassion to describe the grace and nature of God. He told story after story of a God who was nourishing, life giving, embracing, and loving. Jesus knew God to be compassionate both through personal experience and through his encounter with the words of the prophets.

In many ways Jesus brought the words of the prophets to life. He took on the role of the suffering servant described by Isaiah. He shared the prophet's commitment to the poor and the oppressed. He even appeared to accept Isaiah's simple solution to the problem—share your bread. Listen to these words from Isaiah, words Jesus certainly remembered:

> Is not this the fast that I choose:
> to loose the bonds of injustice,
> to undo the thongs of the yoke,
> to let the oppressed go free,
> and to break every yoke?
> Is it not to share your bread with the hungry,
> and bring the homeless poor into your house;

> when you see the naked, to cover them,
>   and not to hide yourself from your own kin? . . .
> If you offer your food to the hungry
>   and satisfy the needs of the afflicted,
> then your light shall rise in the darkness
>   and your gloom be like the noonday.
> —Isaiah 58:6-7, 10

When the disciples reminded Jesus that it was late in the day and urged him to send the people home in order that they could buy bread, Jesus' response was straight out of Isaiah, "You feed them." After checking the inventory, Jesus blessed and distributed the loaves. Over 5,000 people ate and were satisfied.

Jesus still uses the words of Isaiah to call his followers to offer their food to the hungry and satisfy the needs of the afflicted. In the words of Gandhi, "Bread for myself is a physical problem; bread for my brothers and sisters is a spiritual problem." The goal for Jesus today would be the same, to have all eat and be satisfied.

Too few people today eat and are satisfied. Some are unsatisfied because they have too little to eat and others remain unsatisfied though they gorge themselves.

Society has a name for excessive eating; it is called gluttony. The church, however, is less concerned with the amount of food than it is with the way people eat. Gluttony is eating without a sense of community and it is eating without joy or the presence of God.

> *"Feasting needs and builds community. Gluttony cares little for community."*

Gluttony ought not be confused with feasting. Feasting, to eat gloriously, celebrates God's bounty. "Ho, everyone who thirsts, come to the waters; and you that have no money, come, buy and eat! Come, buy wine and milk without money and without price . . . Listen carefully to me, and eat what is good, and delight yourselves in rich food" (Isa. 55:1-2). In Zorba's categories, this is to turn food into work and good humor.

Feasting with friends can be an act whereby we enjoy the goodness and extravagance of our loving God. People criticized John the Baptist for being an ascetic. No so Jesus. He was charged with being a glutton and drunkard because he enjoyed food, drink, and the company of friends. He did not apologize for excess with food or even when a woman poured a costly jar of ointment on him. Loving excess was a sign of the extravagant love of God for people. Occasional banquets for Jesus were both times of great fellowship and a foretaste of the feast to come, the heavenly feast when the family of God will gather together. Meals brought Jesus closer to friends and to God.

Gluttony connects us neither with others or God. Gluttony is a solitary act that defeats rather than enhances community. Excessive eating is solitary, even if others are present. Feasting needs and builds community. Gluttony cares little for community.

Too much of American eating is done without community. Food is eaten on the run—in airport terminals, automobiles, or in our offices as we attempt to meet a deadline. What has happened to leisurely eating? What has happened to mealtimes when parents and children tell stories of the day's activities?

Recently friends remodeled their kitchen and dining room. They eliminated the table and added stools and a counter because they found that their family of five "just doesn't eat together anymore." The counter, they agreed, was better suited for a family on the go. Once again, form follows function. The more we increase the pace, the less frequently we break bread together. This kind of eating also goes to fat and manure.

Gluttony is not only a sin of excess, it is feasting without balance. For Jesus feasting was naturally accompanied by fasting. Fasting, however, is almost unknown in our culture, even though at one time it was a discipline for the average believer.

> *"Gluttony is a misplaced hunger."*

A few years ago when I suggested that Lent, particularly Ash Wednesday and Good Friday, is an appropriate time to fast, I discovered that not a single person in a group of fifty-five had ever fasted. Most people viewed it as quaint or something practiced only by religious fanatics.

Just as Jesus encouraged the feast, he assumed the fast. He did caution those who fasted to do it cheerfully. "And whenever you fast, do not look dismal, like the hypocrites, for they disfigure their faces so as to show others that they are fasting" (Matt. 6:16).

Our society not only eats excessively, it diets excessively. Anorexia nervosa is the fear of food. Women, particularly young women, suffer from this disease. Interestingly, ancient theologians lumped excessive eating and not eating together. They believed both gave food a false value. Both produced an inordinate interest in eating, though one *appeared* to be not eating. Both made eating a fetish, though the latter may be fixed on as little as a raw carrot. But more to the point, the person who diets to extremes makes eating a solitary experience. God and community are eliminated.

Story after story in the Gospels tell of Jesus eating. Nearly all suggest that community is enhanced when people break bread together. Nearly all suggest that eating is an opportunity to experience the new kingdom or new age which Jesus initiates.

In the story of the loaves and the fishes, all that is taught elsewhere in the Gospels comes together. It began when a few people were willing to share their meager gifts. It was enhanced when everyone was divided into communities, fifties and hundreds. It all came together when God blessed their gifts.

What took place was a combination of manna in the wilderness and the Lord's Supper. People had arrived hungry for an experience with God. Jesus taught them and fed them. (Is that two ways of saying the same thing?) In the experience of eating they discovered community. They discovered that eating was a spiritual experience. Their eating became an experience of the living God.

We are people with a great hunger. There is something gnawing within us. We often fill that hunger with things—clothing, jewelry, or trinkets. Or food. We eat out of boredom or frustration. We eat because it satisfies our longing for something deeper or more meaningful. Gluttony is a misplaced hunger.

Gluttony is turning food into fat and manure. But food is more. It can be the occasion for community. It can be an experience of the divine. It can be the occasion for being met by the Christ. It can't get any better than that.

LUST

Jesus said to [the Samaritan woman], "Go, call your husband, and come back." The woman answered him, "I have no husband." Jesus said to her, "You are right in saying, 'I have no husband'; for you have had five husbands, and the one you have now is not your husband. What you have said is true!" (John 4:16-18)

Settling for Sex

Jesus and his disciples were in the foreign territory of Samaria. Once the capital of the Northern Kingdom, Samaria had now become the home of a people who the Jews viewed as half-breeds and worshipers of a false god. The Samaritans called the city in our story Shechem, which means oak. The Jews called this same town Sychar, meaning drunkenness, which tells us what the Jews thought of Samaritans.

Wearied from his journey, Jesus decided to rest from the noon sun and get a drink of water from the well. Soon a woman came to draw water. Why did the woman choose that well when there was a spring 300 yards closer to the city, where she could draw water without pulling up a 1500 foot rope? And why was she drawing water at noon? The normal time for such chores was morning or evening.

Not long into the conversation we begin to understand what Jesus immediately knew. The woman was a whore and the other women of the village would not let her draw from the main village spring.

Have you noticed how frequently prostitutes are depicted as sensitive and perceptive in modern stories? Let us not romanticize this woman. She was hard and tough. She had had five husbands and was now a partner in an illicit affair. Her callousness is evident in her taunt, "How is it that you, a Jew, ask a drink of me, a woman of Samaria?"

Jesus responded, "If you knew the gift of God, and who it is that is saying to you, 'Give me a drink,' you would have asked him, and he would have given you living water." Later he adds, "Everyone who drinks of this water will be thirsty again, but those who drink of the water that I will give them will never be thirsty. The water that I will give will become in them a spring of water gushing up to eternal life" (John 4:10, 14).

Here is a woman who attempted to satisfy herself with a half dozen relationships and found each equally unfulfilling. Water is an apt metaphor for sexual hunger. People today find plenty to drink, but so little that satisfies.

> *"Lust listens to the pop singer cry, 'I want you, I need you, I love you,' and assumes all three say the same thing."*

Today we can talk about sex frankly and portray it openly. Sexual experiences appear to have increased in numbers, but have we made any progress in the areas of intimacy or love? A character in a Graham Greene novel may have been speaking for a whole generation when he confessed that he knew the mechanics of sexual intercourse, but he knew nothing about how to love.

People seek love but far too many end up settling for titillation, which is at best a poor cousin. People want intimacy, but settle for sex. When things are balanced, sex and intimacy are woven together; when they are not, sex is separated from love. When the macho hunk on TV says,

"Wanna make love?" can you tell whether he wants exercise or intimacy?

In earlier days the church used to describe this behavior as lust. Lust, of course, is not a casual glance or a fleeting thought but an uncontrolled sexual passion.

> "Love endures all things; lust endures very little."

Love consists of many things, including friendship, empathy, sympathy, as well as passion. Lust bypasses everything else and moves directly to passion. In so doing, lust produces bad sex because it eliminates relationships and turns the other person into an object or a thing. Lust listens to the pop singer cry, "I want you, I need you, I love you," and assumes all three say the same thing.

The pornography industry feeds on lust. Pornography may even be antisexual or at best asexual because it distorts sex by trivializing it.

"Love never ends," Paul writes in I Corinthians. Lust, on the other hand, has no lasting quality. Whereas love is a marathon runner, lust runs the ten-yard dash. Lust is based on desire, not commitment. It originates in the loins, not the heart. Love endures all things; lust endures very little.

As a society we pay a terrible price for lust. Lust is the parent of thousands of unwanted babies. Lust, the impatient desire, frequently leads to abortion, the quick solution. Lust has contributed to the epidemic of sexually transmitted diseases—gonorrhea, herpes, syphilis, and now the deadly AIDS virus.

There is something quite sad when a mass of people confuse sex and love. Our national obsession with sex trivializes it. Rather than making sex more important, it makes it cheaper. When lust replaces love, fidelity and commitments are pushed aside. Lust is a misplaced effort to find that which is enduring. Malcolm Muggeridge has written, "Today people have sex on their minds, which if you think of it, is a strange place to have it."

Sex is a beautiful plant, but it grows best when it is planted in the soil of commitment and fidelity, not desire and raw passion.

Moses, so the story goes, came down from the mountain with two tablets under his arm. "I've got good news and bad news," he told the people. "The good news is that we held God to ten. The bad news is adultery is still in there."

Actually, the inclusion of "thou shalt not commit adultery" is good news. Its purpose is not to eliminate our fun, but to protect one of God's greatest gifts, the gift of love and family. Lust and adultery are enemies of marriage and family, the Scriptures contend. Fidelity and permanence are the proper conditions for love to grow. It is within the framework of promise that sex becomes more than physical and that love can blossom and flourish.

Nor is it just any kind of marriage that will engender love. Paul writes in Ephesians that husband and wife are to be subject to one another out of their reverence for Christ. The husband *gives* himself to the wife as Christ *gave* himself to the church. The wife likewise *gives* herself to her husband. Only in a permanent relationship, a relationship based on fidelity and giving, can love be nurtured so that the two become one flesh. So important is this union between woman and man that Paul sees it as a mystery tied into the meaning of the relationship between God and his people, between Christ and the church. The union in marriage is like the union between Father, Son, and Holy Spirit.

Jesus senses that the marvelous gift of sex has brought no satisfaction to the Samaritan woman, just as it often does not bring satisfaction in our culture. There is plenty to drink, but people are still thirsty.

Jesus' way of dealing with the Samaritan woman is instructive for us. At no time did he condemn her. At no time did he speak condescendingly to her. He addressed her with candor and warmth. Unlike the fanatics of our day, Jesus is not so much angry at the Samaritan woman as he is sad. He led her toward a new way of life not by ridiculing her present status, but by showing her a more excellent way. He offered to replace the old and inferior with that which was new and better. He offered her the kind of drink, "living water," that would act like an internal percolator, bubbling up, and finally, satisfying her deepest need and deepest thirst.

Paul introduces his great hymn of love in I Corinthians with these words, "But strive for the greater gifts. And I will show you a still more excellent way" (I Cor. 12:31). Jesus offers to show us a more excellent way by transforming our lust into love, our temporary desire into permanent commitment. Wherever he meets us he offers us a new option. The new option is based on his commitment to us, a commitment deep and lasting. For some people this is both exciting and frightening, for it not only means new possibilities, but it means separating from that which is old and familiar. He invites those whose lives are bound by the things they own to become free by giving and sharing. He invites those who are possessed by anger and the desire for revenge to live with forgiveness. He invites those enchained by lust to be freed by his love.

Some hear this invitation and find it too terrifying. Others, like the woman in our story, are captured by his love and liberated by his offer. This woman's life was turned around. Where she once led others to sin, she now led them to Christ. Where once she drank and was not satisfied, now she could say: "Come, see the one who quenched my thirst."

ASH WEDNESDAY

A Second Chance

arry Perkins had that fresh-off-the-farm look when he left home to go to college. Tall and muscular with a smile as big as his father's back forty, Larry was admired and respected by students and faculty alike. His dad, Edgar, often boasted, "Larry has never given me a sleepless night. He's as strong as an ox and as gentle as a kitten."

In his second year at college, Larry began to hang around with a fraternity known for its wild parties. He was seldom a participant in the group's antics, but he seemed to enjoy watching others let off steam.

One Friday night, when the guys were drinking at a county park, a gang of townies crashed the party. They taunted the members of the fraternity, calling them a variety of names. A small scuffle broke out, one of the frat boys got pushed to the ground and Larry came out of the shadows. In an awesome display of strength he broke the nose of one boy, left a terrible gash in the face of another, and smashed in the windows of two cars.

The police were called and Larry was booked for assault and malicious destruction of property. The judge noted that Larry had not provoked the incident and that he was a first offender, but he refused to condone Larry's violence. After a stern warning, the judge assigned Larry to substance abuse counseling and put him on probation. His parents were mortified. The family decided to tell no one about the incident, and since it happened nearly 140 miles away from home, they were certain they could keep it as "their little secret."

When school was out in May, Larry returned home where he got a job working on construction. In mid-June he began to date Monica Froiland, a woman he had long admired from afar. Never in his wildest dreams had he thought that anyone as lovely as Monica would ever be interested in him.

Things began slowly, with Monica a bit reluctant, but before the summer was over they were together every night. They enjoyed doing simple things together. Some nights they went window-shopping at the downtown stores, buying each other imaginary gifts. Other times they sat on the grass in her backyard and found star pictures in the sky. Mostly they talked. He told her everything about his life at home and school, everything except the events of that one horrible night. If Monica knew he had a record, or that he was forced to go through substance abuse counseling, he knew their relationship would be over. Even if she understood, he was certain that her father and mother would not. Peter Froiland, Monica's father, was a respected math teacher at the high school, the teacher Larry admired more than any other.

In August, for the first time in his life, Larry had trouble sleeping. He frequently felt depressed. Lois Perkins noticed the change in her son and suggested he talk to Pastor Smith. "You've always been close to him," she reminded the young man.

Larry wanted to talk to his pastor, but he was afraid that his friend would be hurt and disappointed. When he closed his eyes he could imagine the pastor shaking his head and saying, "Why, Larry? Why?"

In the fall Larry and Monica returned to separate

schools. Larry moved off campus and selected a new group of friends. He no longer drank and he attended chapel every week. Most of the time he felt fine, except when he talked to Monica on the phone. Following their conversations he always felt depressed. This went on all fall.

> *"Why does everyone think Christians will be surprised at sin?"*

The young couple could hardly wait for Christmas vacation, but when December 20 finally came Larry was very uncomfortable. Even though he felt closer to Monica than ever before, he realized that there was a terrible barrier between them. Each time he visited her house during vacation he broke out in a sweat. It was a relief to go back to school.

On Ash Wednesday Larry's roommate invited him to attend the Episcopal church at 7:15 A.M. Perhaps it was because he was in a strange church with a strange liturgy, but Larry was deeply moved by this special service. He nearly wept when the priest put ashes on his forehead with the words, "You are dust and to dust you shall return."

The service seemed to be directed to Larry, because he felt like dust. Like dirt. Though he only caught snatches of the sermon, words about confession, he was visibly shaken when the communion service began. He was certain that the phrase "given and shed for you for the forgiveness of sin" was directed to him.

As he left the church in silence, Larry knew he was living a lie and that he had to do something about it. That evening Monica called to tell him she was coming for the weekend. "I'll be there Friday noon. I'm riding with my cousin Steve, and I'm staying with my friend Ann at the dorm."

When Monica arrived, a depressed and troubled Larry Perkins greeted her. She had never seen him so troubled. Immediately they found a place to be alone.

"I don't even know where to begin," he began weakly. At first the words came out haltingly and jumbled. Finally, he gained some composure and managed to blurt out the entire story, how he had lost control of himself, how he had hurt the other boys and smashed the car. "Everyone was frightened of me," he sobbed, "and I was frightened of myself. I was like a crazy animal. I'm ashamed of everything I did. I'm ashamed that I have deceived you and I don't blame you if you never want to see me again."

Monica took his hand. "I love you," she said simply. "And I have known about your misadventures since we started dating." Larry stared at her in disbelief. "Dad told me," she continued. "He warned me that you were probably going to have a tough summer. At first I was shocked. I told Dad that I could never trust a man who had a violent temper."

Monica paused to wipe the tears that flowed down Larry's cheeks. "The day after Dad first told me about your trouble, he asked me to take a walk with him. Along the way he told me about two incidents early in his life, before he was married. He said, 'Long ago I shared these stories with your mother, but I've waited for the right moment to tell you girls. Now seems like as good a time as any to tell you about what I have done.' He concluded by saying, 'Like all of God's children, Larry deserves a second chance.'"

Monica kissed Larry lightly on the cheek. "I remember saying to Dad, 'Are you telling me that Larry is basically a good person?' And he said, 'Larry is a good person, but like all of us, he is also a sinner. Monica, every person you date is a person in need of God's forgiveness.'"

"I then asked Dad if I should raise the issue with you. He advised me to wait until you were ready to tell me. The last time we talked about this was at Christmas when Dad said, 'Is Larry still carrying that big weight on his back? I hope he'll give it up so he can start walking straight again.'"

The two sat together holding hands. After a long silence Monica said, "I have memorized a lot of scriptures about forgiveness. Would you like to hear some?"

Larry managed a smile while dabbing his eyes. "I never dreamed we'd end up sharing Bible verses together, but I'm ready for anything."

"If we confess our sins, God is faithful and just and will forgive us our sins and cleanse us from all unrighteousness."

Larry nodded, "I ought to know that one. They say it Sunday mornings after confession."

> *"It is our glorious privilege to declare to all we meet that God is more ready to forgive than we are to ask."*

Monica smiled again. "Whoever is in Christ is a new creature. The old has passed away; behold the new has come."

Larry said, "Do you really believe that we can become new?"

Monica said, "I believe that when you have the past forgiven, past sins eliminated, that today can be a new day. It is like Dad said, without forgiveness we carry a ten pound weight." She paused and looked at Larry's massive body. "In your case it is probably a fifty pound weight."

Larry said, "I guess Lent is about as good a time as any

to start over. Pastor Smith used to call Lent a time for spring cleaning. I guess he meant that if you confess those sins, God can sweep them out."

"And," Monica added, "if you confess them, no one can hold them over you again. You are free."

Larry frowned. "I'm going to have a talk with your folks."

"How about Pastor Smith?"

"Absolutely not," Larry said emphatically. "He'll be heartbroken. He'll never respect me again."

Monica said quietly. "He knows."

Larry was astonished. "He never treated me any different!"

Monica's eyes flashed. "Why does everyone think Christians will be surprised at sin? He understands, because, like my dad, he's also a sinner. My hunch is the only one left to forgive Larry, is Larry."

Lent is a time when we are invited to face our sins, confess them, and to be freed from them. We do this by focusing our attention on the One who gave his life so that we need not carry the burdens of yesterday around on our shoulders. It is our glorious privilege to declare to all we meet that God is more ready to forgive than we are to ask. It is our privilege to do this because, as Paul said, we have been entrusted with the message of reconciliation. We are ambassadors for Christ; God makes his appeal through us. Remember, whoever is in Christ is a new creature (II Cor. 5:19-20).

GOOD FRIDAY

God's No

A young woman holding a baby in one arm
  and hanging onto a squirming three year old
    with the other
    stopped me in the hall after church school.
  "I've just read the first two chapters
    of a wonderful book," she said.
  "Do you know about it?
  It is called, *I'm OK, You're OK.*"

I told her that I read the book about twenty years ago.
  "What do you find wonderful about it?" I asked.

She thought for a moment.
  "I like the title.
  I guess I would like it to be true."

So do I.
  I really do.
    But it isn't.

I knew it wasn't true even before I spent seven weeks
  reflecting on the Seven Deadly Sins.

I knew it from reading the papers:
  congressman faces charges of influence peddling,

five weekend homicides in Detroit,
college counselor says 30 percent of all students
   on his campus of 16,000 have an alcohol related
    problem,
major league ball player says he is insulted
   by his $3.5 million contract,
study says 51 percent of all husbands have been
   unfaithful.

I knew it by looking at myself.
  Envy
    pride
      anger
        lust
are not dusty old terms used only by theologians.
They are words that describe my life.
They are words that describe the experiences
   that damage marriages
             friendships
             businesses.

Gluttony
  greed
    sloth
are reasons a life hangs by a thread.
They are indeed deadly sins.

In a single week I see lives broken by
  jealousy
    pettiness
      infidelity.
I visit the hospital to pray with people:
  a man in the cancer ward,
  a teenager in the mental health unit,
  a woman with chronic pain,
  a young boy severely burned.

We are a broken people
     broken bodies
     broken marriages
     broken promises
     broken spirits.

I'm OK—You're OK?

What do we do about our situation?
   Ignore it?
     Get depressed over it?
       Pull ourselves up by our bootstraps?

Of the three, the bootstraps method seems best.
   At least we'd be trying to do something positive.
   And think of the resources to help us.
   A quick trip to the bookstore finds volumes telling
     how to fix our marriages
               sex lives
               friendships
               jobs
               mental health
               finances.

The answer is
   improved attitude
   new information
   better government
   greater spirituality
   more effective communication skills
   an enhanced technology
   more exercise
   heightened self-esteem.

There is something appealing about self-help.
   There is also something noble.
   At least we aren't wading in self-pity.

But there is also something pathetic.
It doesn't work.
For all the great solutions, we are not getting better.
We're just writing more books.

The world of Jesus wasn't a lot different than our world.
There was poverty
discrimination
slavery
brutality
hunger.

And there were solutions to the problems:
more discipline
more order
more education
more religion.
A lot of the answers were of the self-help variety.

Good Friday is a response to all human attempts to save
oneself.
The cross is God's answer to self-help.
It is a one-word answer.
NO!
The cross is God's NO to the assumption that all we need is
new insight
more information
a new skill.

To those who say, "What we need is better education,"
the cross replies—
Jesus was killed by the brightest and the best.
It was the highly educated who plotted his death,
who urged Pilate to nail him to the tree.

To those who say, "What we need is good government,"
the cross replies—

the order to execute came from the Roman Governor,
 a man who worked for one of the most effective
  systems of government ever devised,
 a government that brought "The Pax Romana,"
  peace and stability, to the whole Mediterranean
  world.

To those who say, "Religion is the answer,"
 the cross replies—
  it was the religious authorities who silenced Jesus.
  There was nothing more noble and more advanced
   than Jewish religion.

To those who say, "Economics is the answer,"
 the cross replies—
  it was the wealthy who put Jesus to death.

To those who say, "We need to become kinder people,"
 the cross replies—
  those who hung Jesus were not thugs.
  In most areas of their lives they were decent, caring,
   family men.

On the cross, all of the world's best efforts
 were hung with Jesus.
 We are in bondage to sin and cannot free ourselves.
 We cannot free ourselves by the practice of religion
  (if we understand religion to be our efforts)
 nor by education
 nor by good government
 nor by new technology
 nor even by trying harder.

The cross says we humans are powerless over our condition.
 We will not be right
  until we get right with God

until we turn our lives over to God
until we say—I can't do it
    —help me God
    —your will be done.

In short, we, along with Christ, must die before we live.
  Only those who lose their lives will find it.
  "Unless a grain of wheat falls into the earth and dies,
    it remains alone;
    but if it dies it bears much fruit."
  The cross is the end of human achievement as a way of life.
  At the cross we confess that all of the answers
    of the world are empty.
  Society does not have the answer to security
                   identity
                   well being.

  Until we give up our attempts to save ourselves through
    education
    work
    entertainment
    government
    wealth
  we merely spin our wheels.

It is God alone who can save us.
  And, the gospel tells us, God does.
    God saves us through suffering love.
    God saves us by taking the world's best punch
      its most terrible form of punishment
      and transforming it into forgiveness.
  What they meant for evil, God meant for good.

We can't get it right until we get it right with God.
  And we can't get it right with God until we let God be God.

That means, stop trying to save ourselves
        stop trying to fix ourselves
        stop trying to heal ourselves.

Saving
  fixing
    healing is God's work.

We start by giving up all of our ifs:
  If we only have more time off, it will get better,
  If we learn a bit more
     communicate better
     have more self-pride
     learn new skills
  we can become whole.
  The cross says: none of this works.
  The cross is the end to all ifs.

At the cross we learn what God does to sin.
  He says NO to it.
  He tells us how devastating it is.
  On the cross he demonstrates how it separates us
    from all that is good and godly.
  Then he kills it
      crucifies it
      forgives it.
Through the Righteous One, the Savior,
    God bears the sin of the world.
  He does what we cannot do.

The world is in terrible shape.
  It is full of hurt
        anger
        shame
        pain
        sickness.

We need help.
  We cannot do it ourselves.
  And we need not.
  God has done it for us.
    Jesus died to sin so that we could live to God.

The cross is God's NO to our attempts to save ourselves.
The cross is God's commitment to human beings.
The cross is God's response to our sin
                              our bleak condition.
The cross is God's way of saying I love you
      to a broken world.

I'm OK—you're OK?
  No.

Try this:
  I'm not OK
    You're not OK
      But that's OK.

Thanks be to God.

EASTER SUNDAY

But he said to them, "Do not be alarmed; you are looking for Jesus of Nazareth, who was crucified. He has been raised; he is not here." (Mark 16:6)

God's Yes

It is time, some experts tell us, for churches to accentuate the positive. People are tired of the negative. People are looking for hymns, liturgy, and sermons that are upbeat. What is suggested? Substitute songs of praise for the penitential hymns of Lent. De-emphasize such things as sin and death. One of these experts summarized this position by saying, "We need less Good Friday in our churches, and more Easter."

Easter is good news. Easter is positive, unless you read Mark's story of Easter. Then, let the listener who comes only to hear good news beware. In Mark's Gospel you have to look beneath the surface to find God's word of hope. Mark tells us that Easter, like Good Friday, has elements of terror and dread.

For the first eight verses Mark's Easter story seems positive enough. Initially, the story seems to suggest that the fortitude missing in the men who betrayed and denied Jesus can be found in the women. While the male disciples were still cowering behind closed doors because they feared the Jews, the women began to take care of business. In accord with Jewish custom, they purchased oil to anoint the body of Jesus. Then, before the sun rose, they walked to the place of his burial. Finding the stone rolled away, they boldly entered the tomb.

What they saw terrified them. On the right side of the tomb sat a young man dressed in a white robe. But he was no ordinary human; he was, literally, out of this world. He was a heavenly messenger.

"Do not be alarmed," he said reassuringly. How often in scripture have we heard these or similar words from the mouth of an angel? "Fear not" is the greeting of the heavenly messengers to Elizabeth, Mary, and the shepherds prior to the birth of Jesus. But despite the words of the angels, the almost universal experience of a person when they are in the presence of the divine is somewhere between terror and awe.

"You are looking for Jesus of Nazareth, who was crucified," the angel said. "He has been raised; he is not here. Look, there is the place they laid him." And then he concluded. "But go, tell his disciples and Peter that he is going ahead of you to Galilee; there you will see him, just as he told you" (Mark 16:6-7).

Isn't it ironic that it was women, the ones Jewish society did not allow to be witnesses in court because they were not believed to be truthful, who were the first witnesses of the resurrection? If the world is to know that Jesus is risen from the dead it must come from them. In the new kingdom, "gossips" are transformed into heralds and evangelists.

Actually, the irony just adds spice to what is a pleasant, positive story. At least it is pleasant and positive until we read the last sentence. "So they went out and fled from the tomb, for terror and amazement had seized them; and they said nothing to anyone, for they were afraid" (Mark 16:8).

And now, as one radio commentator says, you know the rest of the story. They blew it, just like the men. The reassuring words of the young man in white weren't enough. Fear overcame them. The story ended on a downer. It ended with a big no!

The biblical story deals with fear because so often our lives are touched by fear. Some fear is understandable. If someone holds a gun to your head, you have every right to be afraid. During our lifetime we face real threats to the well-being of ourselves and those we love. Christians are not asked to be totally fearless.

But there is much that brings fear to us that is foolish. When false fear prevents us from moving ahead, taking risks, when it means that we are reduced to inaction, we experience what the church calls "faintheartedness." False fear paralyzes us. It prevents us from using our talents and gifts.

> *"At times we become functional atheists."*

Easter is not the only biblical story that addresses fear. Do you remember how reluctant Moses was to go back to Egypt to tell Pharaoh to let God's people go? The Lord answered Moses' fear with these brief words, "I am with you."

At the end of the Exodus, in a story found in the first chapter of Deuteronomy, God directed the people of Israel to leave the mountain and cross into the hill country of the Amorites. "See, the Lord your God has given the land to you; go up, take possession, as the Lord, the God of your ancestors, has promised you; do not fear or be dismayed" (Deut. 1:21).

But the people hung back. First they wanted to study the issue. They appointed a committee. When the committee reported that everything was OK, they still wanted to wait for favorable conditions. They were frightened; they were fainthearted.

Moses understood their reluctance as a lack of faith in

God. Faintheartedness comes from the belief that we walk alone. It denies the ability of God to guide and protect us.

Jesus exposed such anxiety with these words, "Therefore I tell you, do not worry about your life, what you will eat or what you will drink, or about your body, what you will wear. Is not life more than food, and the body more than clothing? Look at the birds of the air; they neither sow nor reap nor gather into barns, and yet your heavenly Father feeds them. Are you not of more value than they?" (Matt. 6:25-26).

We often live as if we are of less value than birds. We live as if God cannot do anything to assist us. We let minor decisions in our lives fill us with anxiety. At times we become functional atheists, living in fear of the most simple decisions of vocation, travel, or family. Despite the words of Jesus, we fret about what we will eat or what we will wear. We stew about tomorrow, forgetting today's trouble is enough for today.

Some worry, particularly for older adults, is fueled by the incessant violence on television. They suffer from "The Mean World Syndrome," living in fear, believing society to be a dark and forbidding place. They can't have enough locks on their doors and they trust few people on the streets. They live as if God has abandoned them to suffer in this world.

In a world full of fear and anxiety, people want a word of hope. When so many things say no, you and I want something to say yes.

And you and I will hear it on this Easter morning. We will hear it in the face of the world's no. We will hear it in the face of anxiety and fear. God's yes comes not only as an answer to society's no, but as an answer to the Lenten stories of betrayal, denial, and fear. It comes in the midst of the story of men hiding and women fleeing in "terror and amazement."

The first yes of Easter is found in the words of the angel

to the women, "Go, tell his disciples and Peter that he is going ahead of you to Galilee; there you will see him, just as he told you." This is the word of Jesus to the people who fell asleep as he prayed in the garden. This is the word of Jesus to those who denied him, or betrayed him, or fled in fear when the enemy came. This word says, "Despite all that you have done, you are still in my plans. You are still my friends. You have not been abandoned."

> *"Easter is God's yes to the weak and the faint-hearted. And therefore it is God's yes to us."*

The story of the disciples of Jesus is no different from the story of Israel. Both were a stiff-necked people. The disciples denied and abandoned their master because they refused to let God's way be their way. They misunderstood his teaching about children, money, and the poor. They interrupted him at prayer, tried to silence beggars who called out to be healed, and turned away parents who brought young children to him.

And still he loved them. Still he cared for them. Easter is God's yes to the weak and the fainthearted. And therefore it is God's yes to us. In the words of Edmund Steimle, "One of the mysteries of Easter is . . . that we can rejoice and sing our hallelujahs—at the moment that we are shown up for what we really are and have been."

We are often afraid that if someone really knows us, they won't like us. Easter declares that God knows everything about us and still loves us. God knows our pride, our envy, our greed and still calls us his children. God has witnessed our anger, our lust, and our apathy and continues to treat us as his prized possession.

Envy and pride separate us from our neighbors and

God. Apathy and anger isolate and divide us from the earth and the rest of the human family. Our sin puts us in the far country. But God who loves us is not content to let us remain isolated. We who were "far off have been brought near by the blood of Christ" (Eph. 2:13). Easter is God's way of calling us home.

At Easter, we all—first and twentieth century disciples—discover the truth of Paul's great declaration, "Nothing can separate us from the love of God." Nothing. Not death, not anything in life, not supernatural powers, not our own foolish sin and fear, nothing in all creation is able to separate us from the love of God in Christ Jesus our Lord.

Easter begins as God's yes to Jesus. At Easter God says yes to the way Jesus lived. God says yes to the way of love, the way of forgiveness, the way of nonviolence. In the resurrection God says, "The way of Jesus is my way." At Easter God highly exalted him and gave him a name above every name.

Easter is God's yes in the face of death. At Easter God says, "Because I live, you too will live." God's yes is spoken to a world of death, a world in which more people die on the streets of our American cities than in all of Desert Storm. It is spoken to a world where cancer and heart attacks and accidents can strike at any moment.

So many things say no, but Easter says yes. Yes to life. Yes to life beyond life.

To all of you who are tired of the world's no, we send you home today with God's yes. Here is the way Norman Habel has put it.

> And God said, Yes! Yes! Yes!
> Said Yes to the world once more.
> Said Yes with a cosmic roar,
> Said open that other door,
> Said Yes! Yes! Yes!

GOD'S YES

For God said, Yes! Yes! Yes!
Yes to His broken son!
Yes to His open wound!
Yes to the broken tomb!
Said Yes, Yes, Yes

And God said Yes! Yes! Yes!
We'll leap the swirling sky!
We'll leap the hungry grave
We'll never stop to die.
God says Yes! Yes! Yes!

Amen.